WITHDRAWN

P9-DVY-501

THE FOLKLORE
of
WEDDINGS
and
MARRIAGE

THE
Traditional Beliefs
Customs, Superstitions, Charms
AND
Omens of
MARRIAGE
and Marriage Ceremonies

Selected and Edited by
DUNCAN EMRICH

Illustrated by
TOMIE DE PAOLA

American Heritage Press
New York
A Subsidiary of McGraw-Hill

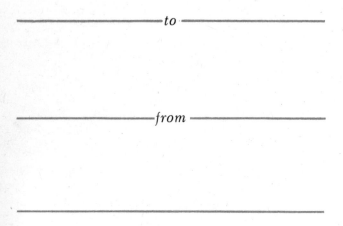

to

from

INTRODUCTION

With one or two rare exceptions, all the marriage customs and wedding traditions in these pages have been found in the United States, and some few are purely American. The majority, however, have their roots in England and Scotland, while a goodly number have ultimate sources in Anglo-Saxon times and in the days of Greece and Rome. The folk beliefs have come down over the centuries—marriage ceremony after marriage ceremony, wedding after wedding, bride after bride after bride. Not all are to be implicitly followed today, but few are to be wholly ignored. Pick and choose, but follow some. Time is on their side and will continue to be. It would be utter folly—on *the* day—to throw all tradition out the window. You can wager the new dime in the heel of your left shoe that your grandmother didn't, and your daughter won't!

And may the day be a "pretty day!"

—D.E.

Dear, dear doctor,
What will cure love
Nothing but the clergy,
And white kid glove.

When a chicken comes into the house with a piece of straw in its beak and lays it down, there will be a wedding soon.

＊

A cow lowing during the night is a sign of an approaching wedding.

＊

When a mockingbird flies over the house, or when a white dove comes near the house, someone is going to be married.

＊

When a spider spins down from the ceiling on his thread, go and "dance him up and down," and there will be a wedding.

Feed a cat out of an old shoe, and your wedding day will be a happy one.

*

If a cat sneezes in front of a bride on the day before her wedding, it is a sign of very good luck.

*

It is good luck for a bride to dream of her wedding day.

*

It is bad luck for a bride to read the marriage service on the day before her wedding, and it is bad luck also for her to rehearse the wedding.

*

You should not marry a man whose surname begins with the same letter as your own:

> *Change the name and not the letter,*
> *Change for worse and not for better.*

It is unlucky to marry someone born in the same month as your own.

❋

Marry in May,
You'll rue the day.

❋

Married in the month of June,
Life will be one honeymoon.

Marry when the year is new,
Always loving, kind, and true.
When February birds do mate,
You may wed, nor dread the fate.
If you wed when March winds blow,
Joy and sorrow both you'll know.
Marry in April when you can,
Joy for maiden and for man.
Marry in the month of May,
You will surely rue the day.
Marry when June roses blow,
Over land and sea you'll go.
Those who in July do wed,
Must labor always for their bread.
Whoever wed in August be
Many a change are sure to see.
Marry in September's shrine,
Your living will be rich and fine.
If in October you will marry,
Love will come, but riches tarry.
If you wed in bleak November,
Only joy will come, remember.
When December's snows fall fast,
Marry and true love will last.

The belief that June is the happiest month for marriage goes back to the days of Rome. Juno—wife of Jupiter, patroness of the young, and goddess of marriage—is especially honored at this time. The Romans felt that prosperity came to the man and happiness to the maid married then. May, on the other hand, is named for Maia, goddess of growth and patroness of the old. It is a month which honors the unhappy dead.

In his *Almanack* for the year 1655, Andrew Waterman, mariner, lists the following days "whereon it is good to marry, or contract a Wife, for then Women will be fond and loving":

January 2, 4, 11, 19, 21	July 1, 3, 12, 19, 21, 31
February 1, 3, 10, 19, 21	August 2, 11, 18, 20, 30
March 3, 5, 12, 20, 23	September 1, 9, 16, 18, 28
April 2, 4, 12, 20, 22	October 1, 8, 15, 17, 27, 29
May 2, 4, 12, 20, 23	November 5, 11, 13, 22, 25
June 1, 3, 11, 19, 21	December 1, 8, 10, 19, 23, 29

Marry in Lent,
You'll live to repent.†

It will bring you bad luck to marry on your birthday.

† The church considered all penitential days throughout the year unsuitable for the joyous ceremony of marriage.

In Scotland, the thirty-first of December is a most popular day for weddings. The whole world celebrates with you, and by the following morning you will have been happily married for a year. For the rest of your married life you are certain of celebrations on your wedding anniversary (an anniversary which becomes impossible for a husband to forget), and the following day brings in again the double New Year of time and wedded time.

*

The day of the week upon which the fourteenth of May falls is deemed unlucky, throughout the entire rest of the year, for marriage or the transaction of any important business. If it falls on Monday, all Mondays from then on are unlucky; on Tuesday, all Tuesdays; on Wednesday . . .

Wed on Monday, always poor,
Wed on Tuesday, wed once more,
Wed on Wednesday, happy match,
Wed on Thursday, splendid catch,
Wed on Friday, poorly mated,
Wed on Saturday, better waited.

*

Monday for health,
Tuesday for wealth,
Wednesday the best day of all,
Thursday for losses,
Friday for crosses,
And Saturday no luck at all.

Be sure that the marriage ceremony is completed between the half hour and the hour. The rising hand of the clock denotes success and rising fortune, while any wedding performed after the hour, when the hand is falling, bears an omen of falling fortune and failure.

*

The same holds true for the moon. Falling fortune and failure comes with a waning moon. Marry when the moon is on the increase and, at the very best, when it is almost full.

*

Marry also with a rising, rather than an ebbing, tide, if you live along the seacoast. From the Orkney Islands: *"No couple chuses to marry except with a growing Moon, and some even wish for a flowing tide."*

Wed in the morning,
Quickly undoing.

*

Late morning and afternoon weddings are best.

*

In the seventeenth century, morning weddings were strongly deplored for the reason that the bridegroom was apt to appear "unshaven and wearing dirty or negligent attire," as the result either of early morning work in the country or of a last round of all-night bachelor parties in the city.

*

Evening weddings were also strictly tabooed, but for another reason: the wedding party, as the clergy noted with protective horror, frequently "took the bridal couple off by sheer force to the ale house."

If a drop of rain falls on a bride, or a tear on a new born babe, they will go through life weeping.

*

"If you marry on a pretty day, you will live happy."

*

If it rains on the wedding, the bride will cry all her married life.

*

You will shed a tear for each raindrop that falls on your wedding day.

*

To marry in a storm betokens an unhappy wedded life.

*

It is good luck if a ray of sunshine falls on a bride when she is coming out of the church.

*

Thunder during your wedding signifies unhappiness in your married life.

Happy the bride
The sun shines on,
Woe to the bride
The rain rains on.†

† In earlier days, weddings were celebrated at the church door or in the church porch, not in the body of the church. A wet day, at such a time, was a serious matter, especially since our forefathers did not have modern contrivances—umbrellas, awnings, and such—to protect them from the rain. Church porch and church door weddings were discountenanced in Edward VI's (1537–1553) reign, and Innocent III had ordered weddings to be celebrated in the church as early as the twelfth century. The folk sayings and beliefs have been firmly maintained in tradition, however, to this day.

"If it snows on your wedding day, you will get a dollar for every flake that falls on you."

＊

Snow falling on the wedding day means happiness for the bridal couple.

The wedding day is the bride's day, and the day following is the bridegroom's day. The weather on each foretells their future. If the bride's morning is fair and the afternoon rainy, the first part of her married life will be happy, and the latter part unhappy. The same holds true also for the groom on his day. If the sun shines and there is no rain or storm on either day, both will be happy throughout their married life.

The day after the wedding is called the groom's day, and is also called the "infare" or "infair" day. And in Maine, it is known as "the second-day wedding." On the wedding day itself, the company and guests return to the bride's parents' house for feasting and festivities. On the "infare" day, the bridal couple, with a large party of friends, is entertained with a sumptuous groaning-board dinner at the house of the parents of the groom.

*

"Old people tell, with real joy, of the infair *(or* infare*), the big dinner at the bridegroom's parents' house the next day after the wedding. The couple nearly always spent their first night at the home of the bride's parents; the next day, they and their attendants (usually two couples) came in their buggies to the big dinner. In my youth in Kentucky I remember having attended, as a younger brother, two such celebrations in 1896 and 1903."*

Postponing a wedding is very bad luck.

The postponement of a wedding is an almost certain sign that either the bride or groom will die within a short space of time—a year or two—so that when a date is once decided upon for the marriage, the ceremony must be performed, no matter what the weather conditions may be.

To see a lamb or dove on the way to church is a sign of good luck, but if a pig should cross the path of the carriage, it is a bad omen.

＊

In England it was, and may still be, good luck to see a wolf, spider, or toad, but bad luck to meet a friar, priest, dog, cat, hare, lizard, or serpent.

＊

To see a flock of white birds is a sign of good luck, and a flock of black birds bad. A flock of birds flying directly over the bridal carriage on its way to church signifies that the couple will have many children.

＊

A bride will be unlucky if her carriage on the road to church meets or passes a funeral procession.

It is bad luck for a bride to drop her handkerchief either when stepping into or alighting from her carriage.

*

It is good luck for a bride to carry bread in her pocket, for when she throws it away, she throws away her troubles. For every piece of bread she gives to the poor whom she meets on the way to church, a misfortune is averted.

*

Never hand a telegram to a bride or bridegroom while they are on their way to church. (This is a belief or superstition arising out of common horse sense: if it is merely a congratulatory telegram, it can wait; if it brings news of death or other sorrow or trouble, it should be put aside.)

Married in blue, love ever true,
Married in white,† you've chosen right,
Married in red, you'll wish yourself dead,
Married in black, you'll wish yourself back,
Married in gray, you'll go far away,
Married in brown, you'll live out of town,
Married in green, ashamed to be seen,
Married in pink, of you only he'll think,
Married in pearl, you'll live in a whirl,
Married in yellow, jealous of your fellow.

† White, as the accepted color for the formal wedding, is fairly recent. It is the symbol, of course, of purity and innocence, a symbol which goes back to the days of the Greeks. It was not until the late eighteenth century, however, that white began to be fashionable for the wedding gown, a fashion confirmed in Victorian times, and unchallenged today. For the informal wedding the bride may select any color she considers most suitable, except that red and black—symbols of devilry and witchcraft—are taboo.

> *If when you marry, your dress is red,*
> *You'll wish to God that you was dead;*
> *If when you marry, your dress is white,*
> *Everything will be all right.*

*

A widow may wear black if she puts a rose in her hair, but if the flower falls out, she will lose her second husband.

If a woman marries in red, she will fight with her husband before the year is out, or he will soon die.

*

> *Blue is true,*
> *Yaller's jealous,*
> *Green's forsaken,*
> *Red is brazen,*
> *White is love,*
> *And black is death.*

"It is bad luck for a bride to eat anything while she is adorning for her marriage, or until after the ceremony."

After the bride is completely dressed for the ceremony, she must not look into a mirror until the preacher has pronounced the fateful words. If she does, the marriage will turn out badly. The bride may dress before her mirror, but should be careful to leave off some small item of attire—a ribbon-bow, a flower, a pin— which is added at the last minute without looking in the glass.

*

Wear earrings when you are married, and you will always be happy.

*

It is bad luck for the groom to see the bride in her wedding gown before the actual ceremony.

*

It is bad luck to make your own wedding gown, to tear your wedding gown, or to have wine spilled on it.

It is a sign of very good luck for the bride to find a spider crawling on her wedding dress.

*

Pearls are the symbols of tears. For each pearl that the bride wears, her husband will give her cause for weeping.

A bride must have her hair dressed and her veil put on by a happily married woman.

*

If, at the wedding, you can wear the bridal veil worn by your grandmother, you will always have wealth.

Good luck will come to a bride if her veil is accidentally torn, and particularly if it is accidentally torn at the altar.

*

Bad luck comes to the bride who shows her wedding veil to anyone (members of the family excepted) before the wedding.

*

[The veil itself is Eastern in origin, and the custom of wearing it was introduced into Europe by the returning Crusaders. Eastern women wore it to ward off the evil eye, and it protected not only the face, but the whole body as well. It was not removed until after the wedding ceremony, and the wearing of it to that time was a sign to the groom that the bride was pure and innocent. When the veil was introduced into European and, later, American weddings, the symbolism of this purity and innocence continued to be associated with it. Among the Anglo-Saxons also it was the custom for four tall men to hold a veil or canopy over the bride at her wedding to hide her blushes. If she was a widow, the veil was esteemed useless.]

A bride at her wedding should wear:

> *Something old,*
> *Something new,*
> *Something borrowed,*
> *Something blue,*
> *And a sixpence in the shoe.*

Or, in the United States:

> *. . . And a new dime in the shoe.*

The "old" must be something which has belonged to a happily married woman. The wearing of such an item insures a lucky transfer of happiness to the new **bride**.

The "new" is the wedding gown, the shoes, or other apparel of the bride.

The "borrowed" must be some object of gold to guarantee wealth and fortune in the future.

The "blue" is symbolic of the heavens and also of true love.

The "sixpence" or "new dime" must be worn in the heel of the left shoe to insure wealth and prosperity.

*

New and blue,
Old and gold.

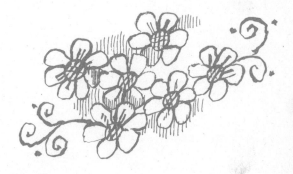

Orange blossoms*are lucky, whether worn by the bride or used in the wedding decorations.

*

A bride will always be happy if she wears or carries a bit of salt in her glove or shoe or pocket when she goes to church to be married. Salt has two exceptional virtues: it is abhorred by witches and devils, and, as a preservative, it has symbolized lasting friendship and loyalty since the days of the Greeks.

*Orange blossoms stand for the greatest good fortune, since they symbolize—according to the Chinese, Greeks, Romans, and the Crusaders who brought them to northern Europe—innocence, purity, lasting love, and fertility, all in one. Because the tree is an evergreen, it symbolizes the lasting nature of love. Because it bears both blossoms and fruit at one and the same time, it symbolizes, in the delicate blossoms, the innocence and purity of young love, and, in the fruit, the proved promise of fertility and motherhood. On her wedding night, Juno was presented with the rarest of gifts, "golden apples." Also, orange blossoms were, until quite recently, enormously expensive and were worn only by the very rich and the very noble in Europe.

The bridegroom should carry a horseshoe in his pocket for good luck. (A miniature one might do.)

*

A bride will have bad luck if she carries a handkerchief used by another bride, but good luck if she carries her mother's prayer book.

Today the bride's bouquet is often one of lilies of the valley, white orchids, white roses, or some other delicate flower. Once it was a combination of garlic, chives, rosemary, bay, and other strong and potent herbs, all carefully selected for their special protective power against witches and demons.

*

At one time also, the bride carried small stalks of wheat, or corn stalks and leaves, to symbolize fruitfulness.

*

And once she also wore laurel leaves in her hair—as a sign of victory! *Amor vincit omnia!*

It is bad luck to have a gray horse at a wedding.

A bat flying into the church during the wedding ceremony is a sign of bad luck.

＊

It is unlucky if a bride does not weep bitterly on her wedding day: *"She takes it by tradition from her Fellow-Gossips, that she must weep shoures upon her Marriage Day: though by the vertue of mustarde and onyons, if she cannot naturally bring them forth."*

＊

A bride who sheds tears on her wedding day will always be happy, for it shows that she has wept all her tears away. The tears shed on that day are the last tears, and beyond that day lies happiness.

If the ring is dropped by the best man or groom before it is placed on the bride's finger, it is most unlucky, just as it is also unlucky for the bride to try the ring on before the ceremony.

*

It is best to purchase a wedding ring from a mail-order house, because the ordinary "store bought" ring may have absorbed bad luck from someone who tried it on in the store.

There are those who believe that once the ring has been placed on the hand, it should never be removed. The phrase in the ceremony, "Till death do us part," seems to have become associated with the ring. Therefore it must remain on the hand until death.

Others believe that if you slip the ring on and off once before leaving church, you will not have bad luck if for any reason it is necessary to remove it later. Some even believe that it brings positive good luck to take the wedding ring off and put it back on just before leaving church.

Another belief has it that it is unlucky to take a wedding ring off your finger until you have been married a year.

And others feel that once on the bride's finger, the ring should not be removed for seven years.

*

> *As the wedding ring wears,*
> *So wear away life's cares.*

In the days of Rome and through the Middle Ages and the Renaissance, only the wealthy wore rings as a matter of course, and it was a sign of nobility and rank to possess one. The single exception allowed to the lower classes was the wedding ring, an indication in itself of the esteem and honor in which it was held.

＊

In the Anglo-Saxon north, rings were originally pledges given to the bride, along with other gifts, before the ceremony of marriage. The word "wed" itself is Anglo-Saxon and means "pledge." "Wedding" comes from it. So that the ring, from Anglo-Saxon usage, is a pledge and a wedding, forever.

＊

The circle of the ring, without end, is the symbol of eternity, and stands for the endless love of the couple.

The reasons given for the wearing of the ring upon
the fourth finger of the left hand are three:

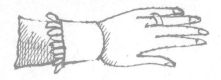

The most practical and mundane is the Roman ex-
planation that this finger best protects the valuable
ring. The left hand, to begin with, is used less than
the right; therefore the ring belongs to the left. And
of the fingers on the left hand, the fourth is the only
one which cannot easily be extended except in the
company of another. The finger is protected: the ring
is as safe as it can be.

The second reason goes back to the Egyptians, who
believed that a vein ran from the fourth finger of the
left hand directly to the heart. Since the heart con-
trolled both life and love, this finger was the most
honored. It deserved the ring, the pledge of love.

The third reason stems from the Christian Church which, to impress the seriousness of the ceremony upon the bride and groom, lectured that the thumb and first two fingers of the hand stood respectively for the Father, the Son, and the Holy Ghost, and that the fourth stood for the earthly love of man for woman, their marriage together, and the hope of Heaven to follow.

"With this rynge I thee wed, and this gold and silver I thee give, and with my body I thee worship, and with all my worldly chatels I thee endow." When the groom had said these words, he held the ring for a moment over the tip of the thumb of the ring hand, saying, "In the name of the Father;" then held it briefly to the tip of the second finger, saying, "And of the Son"; then put it to the tip of the third finger, saying, "And of the Holy Ghost;" and, lastly, placed it firmly on the fourth finger with a resolute "Amen."

A bride must step over the church sill with her right foot. This is true both on entering and leaving the church; and also, when leaving the altar, the bride should put her right foot first for luck and happiness.

*

"If a man and woman get married and the wife steps out of the church with her left foot first, her marriage will be very unsuccessful and will end up in court."

*

At the altar itself, the bride should try to see that her right foot is placed ahead of the groom's. This will insure her future influence over him.

At the wedding, if the bride sees the bridegroom before he sees her, she will always retain her influence over him; but if the bridegroom sees the bride before she sees him, he will always retain his influence over her.

*

When hands are joined during the marriage service, the one whose thumb is on top will be the master of the household.

*

It is important during the service that the bride and groom stand parallel to the planks or cracks of the floor, and not at right angles to them. "If they stand crossways, they'll have a cross life."

As each newly married couple leaves the church, the great bells of Bow ring out:

> *Two more poor fools undone!*
> *Two more poor fools undone!*
> *Two more poor fools undone!*

[It is a matter of love and of record that the great majority of "poor fools" have no desire to undo their undoing.]

Of Rice and Wedding Cakes:

At marriage ceremonies in ancient Rome, the bride held three wheat ears in her left hand, and the priest broke and divided a wheaten cake between the bride and groom. Both were symbols of fertility and fruitfulness.

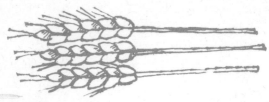

Later, in England, the bride also carried wheat ears
in her hand, or wore upon her head a chaplet of
bearded spikes of wheat. As long as she did so, whole
kernels of wheat and corn were also tossed on her
head when she returned from church. The dry kernels
were picked up and eaten for luck and prosperity by
the guests as well as by uninvited spectators.

This custom flourished well into the middle of the
nineteenth century in England, but then a change
took place. A gentleman, Mr. John Jeaffreson, noted
it in 1872:

> *"My friend, Mr. Moncure Conway, tells me that
> not long since he was present at a wedding in
> London, when rice was poured over the head of
> the bride. The bride and groom of this wedding
> were English people, moving in the middle rank
> of prosperous Londoners."*

This is the first recorded notice of the change from the
traditional country wheat and corn to the now uni-
versally fashionable rice. The use of rice in English
and American weddings dates from this time. The old
symbolism—fertility and fruitfulness—remains, however, with the color now a genteel and matching white.

Rice should be thrown over a bride so that some of it falls in her bosom.

Throw rice after a newly married couple to give them luck, and to increase the chances of their having children.

*

A bride must take no part in the making of her own wedding cake.

"The mother-in-law should break a cake or loaf of bread over the bride's head as she first enters the door of her new home. This will establish friendly relations and make both happy."

The wedding cake evolved side by side with the con-
tinuing custom of tossing corn and wheat over the
bride's head. When some wedding guests lost their
appetite for the dry kernels of wheat, innovators in
pre-Elizabethan times began to make large, thin, dry
biscuits of the grain. These biscuits—wheaten or oat-
meal cakes—were broken over the bride's head, and
the fragments gathered from the ground and distribu-
ted to the guests. (This custom continued in Scotland
well into the nineteenth century.)

The next step toward the modern wedding cake was
to substitute small buns or individual cakes—richly
made with sugar, eggs, milk, spices, and currants—for
the pieces of dry biscuit. In Elizabethan times, these
little bride-cakes were catered and were also brought
in packets by the many guests, so that the quantity of
them was considerable. Some were tossed over the
bride's head as she returned from church, and the rest
were stacked in a high mound on the table, over the
top of which the bride and groom kissed.

A large platter of these square or rectangular blocks continued to be put before the English bride from the Elizabethan period until the Restoration under Charles II in 1660. On Charles' return from exile in France, French chefs and French pastry cooks followed along to serve the English court in London. It was they who achieved the completion of the wedding cake in the 1660's: they simply iced the pile of solid squares with an outer crust of hardened white sugar, and then topped it with decorative wedding figures and toys. A cake of this sort was not difficult to break —held over the bride's head and the outer crust broken, the inner individual cakes tumbled over her to the ground as readily as though they had never been encased in sugar.

A last step was the creation of two cakes: one "a sumptuous ornament for the bridal table," its tiers still recalling the stacks of separate cakes; and the other a smaller one to be broken according to custom over the girl's head. Today there is still a more practical development—the single imposing wedding cake, plus smaller square blocks, separately made and beribboned, to be given to the guests.

With the rice and the pieces of cake, the old traditions still remain—not too far a cry, if one knows the road, from kernels of wheat and corn, and from dry, thin oaten biscuits.

It is unlucky to give away a wedding present.

*

The bride who breaks something on her wedding day will quarrel with her mother-in-law, and the husband will side with his mother.

The first one of a bridal couple who drinks a glass of water after the ceremony will rule.

*

Give the clergyman an odd sum of money for luck.

If an ex-lover with hatred in his heart kisses the bride on her wedding day, her honeymoon will be an unhappy one.

*

A mother-in-law's test of her new daughter-in-law is to place a broom on the floor. If the bride removes it and places it to one side, she will be a good housewife; if she steps over it, she will be a bad housewife.

The word "bridal" comes from "bride-ale," from the fact that on her wedding day the bride and her family were permitted to sell ale especially made for the occasion. Selling the bride-ale helped defray the cost of the festivities and added to their gaiety.

If the youngest daughter in a family marries before her older sisters, they must dance barefoot at her wedding, or in green stockings. This will bring them husbands. To make the success of this doubly certain, the older sisters should dance in a hog's or pig's trough. *"In the case to which I refer, a brother went through the ceremony also, and the dancers performed their part so well, that they danced both the ends off the trough, and the trough itself fell into two pieces."*

"*In the North of England, the young men, immediately after the ceremony, used to strive to be first in plucking off the bride's garters from her legs. This was done before the very altar; and the bride was generally gartered with ribbons for the occasion. Those who were so fortunate as to be victors in this singular species of contest, during which the bride was very frequently thrown down, bore them about the church in triumph. To prevent this very indecent assault, it was usual for the bride to give garters out of her bosom.*"

*

In Scotland, the piper at a wedding always had a piece of the bride's garter tied about his pipes, and young gallants wore them in their hats as trophies. Superb souvenirs!

The bridesmaid who catches the bride's bouquet will be the first to marry. If the bouquet should fall to the floor without being caught, it is an omen of bad luck for the bride.

When she takes her wedding clothes off, the bride should follow the custom of throwing a stocking over her left shoulder. If it lies in a straight line on the floor, her luck will be continuous. Otherwise, it will be varied and changeable.

*

A bride must throw away and lose the pins from her bridal array. If she keeps even one pin, nothing will go right; and if a bridesmaid keeps a pin, she will not be married for a year.

The throwing of an old shoe after a newly wedded couple brings them luck.

*

"It is good luck forever if the slipper thrown after the bride lights on top of the carriage."

[From earliest times, the symbol of domestic authority has been the shoe. In Anglo-Saxon marriages, the father, to demonstrate transfer of authority over his daughter from himself to the groom, took a shoe off the bride's foot and handed it to the groom. Upon receiving the shoe, the groom became the bride's owner and master. To show his acquisition of authority, he tapped the bride lightly on the head with the sign of power, the shoe. So today, when a slipper or shoe is thrown after the married couple or after their car, it is a symbol of relinquishment of authority on the part of the father of the bride, and a total transfer of that authority and power to the groom. The slipper or shoe should, in carrying out this tradition, be thrown by the father of the bride or by some close relative.]

The honeymoon is "the first sweet month of matrimony," and so named because the Anglo-Saxons were in the habit of drinking mead or honey wine for the first thirty days after marriage.

*

For good luck, a bride must take something borrowed with her on her wedding trip.

*

It is bad luck to sleep in your new house or permanent home on the first night of the wedding.

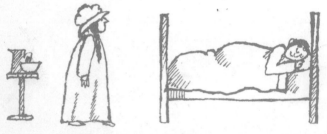

If the husband goes to bed first on the night of the wedding, he will live longer than his wife.

*

The first one to go to sleep on the wedding night will be the first to die.

*

"Take a pound of Limburger cheese, spread between two towels, making a poultice. Place under the pillow of newlyweds on their first night together, and good fortune and many offspring will be theirs."

The bride and bridegroom who sleep with their heads to the north on their wedding night will always be happy.

*

"It is very bad luck for a bride to put her feet on the bare floor on her wedding night. I had always heard this, and on my wedding night I got out of bed forgetting the old saying and put my feet on the bare floor, and I had nothing but bad luck and hell all through my married life."

On the morning following the wedding, the bride has the privilege of asking the husband for any sum of money or piece of property that she pleases. The husband is in honor bound to give it to her.

*

Or, instead, the husband may offer "the morning's gift." The gift, or promise of gift, which he makes to her at this time must be honored, and the property so acquired becomes the separate and exclusive property of the wife, and is the base for her pin money.

It is bad luck for a bride to stumble over the threshold of her new home, an omen of unhappy married
life.

*

The husband must carry the bride over the threshold
of their new home. The Romans believed that she was
most vulnerable at this transitional point in her life,
and that the husband, by carrying her over the sill,
averted any danger from envious witchcraft of the
evil eye.

To protect her new house against witches, the bride
should place a broom and a bowl of salt at the door.
Witches must count the straws in the broom and the
grains of salt before passing beyond them, and since
they are unable to complete this between midnight
and the light of dawn, the house and the people in it
are fully protected.

"It is very bad luck to set up housekeeping with a new coffeepot. Borrow a battered old coffeepot and use it for a month or two, before bringing a brand-new one into the house."

*

"If your husband leaves the house in an angry mood. go to a friend's house and eat applesauce. When he comes home, everything will be forgotten."

*

"Never, never let a man see you undress. It always causes trouble in the family and maybe a divorce."

*

"If your wife becomes angry and tries to fight you, catch and kiss her while she is angry. If you do not, some other man will kiss her before the year is out."

*

"When the husband gets mad, he must take off his hat and turn it around. This will make peace in the family at once."

*

"The fur of a cat blowing the wrong way means that your husband is looking favorably at another woman. This may be counteracted by greasing the fur."

It is a pleasure to acknowledge the following sources: Fanny D. Bergen, *Current Superstitions*, Boston, 1896, and *Animal and Plant Lore*, Boston, 1899; John Brand, *Observations on Popular Antiquities*, London, 1877; Ray B. Browne, *Popular Beliefs and Practices from Alabama*, Berkeley, 1958; Robert Chambers, *Book of Days*, 2 vols., London, 1879; William Hone, *The Every-Day Book and Table Book*, 3 vols., London, 1827, and *The Year Book*, London, 1832; Harry M. Hyatt, *Folklore from Adams County, Illinois*, New York, 1935; John Cordy Jeaffreson, *Brides and Bridals*, 2 vols., London, 1872; Vance Randolph, *Ozark Superstitions*, New York, 1947; T. F. Thiselton-Dyer, *Folklore of Women*, London, 1905; Annie Weston Whitney and Caroline Canfield Bullock, *Folklore from Maryland*, New York, 1925.